This book is dedicated to all of my family members for their support, especially to my wife and mentors who have always taught me every step of my career.

THE STAFFING STORY

HOW WE GOT HERE AND WHERE WE'RE GOING IN THE WORLD OF HIRING

MOHAMMAD ARSHAD

Made with ♥ on the Notion Press Platform
www.notionpress.com

Contents

Preface

The Staffing Story: How We Got Here and Where We're Going in the World of Hiring is a book that reflects my journey in the staffing industry. It is a culmination of my experiences, observations, and insights, which I have gained over the years while working with some of the world's leading companies in the staffing industry.

My career in the staffing industry began during the mid-2000s when India was becoming a hub for IT jobs. I started my career as a Talent Acquisition Specialist, supporting my US clients from India during graveyard shifts. It was a challenging time for me as I had to deal with the time difference, cultural differences, and communication barriers. However, I learned a lot during that time and developed the necessary skills to become a global Talent Acquisition Consultant with extensive knowledge of the staffing industry across the world.

Throughout my career, I have worked with several Fortune 500 companies in the staffing industry, including CSC, Google, Apple, BAE Systems, General Dynamics, UHG, Intel, Deloitte, Boeing Systems, Raytheon, AKQA, Kroger, Facebook, GE, JP Morgan, Amazon, Citigroup, Goldman Sachs, IBM, among others. I have demonstrated expertise in software ERP and infrastructure, coupled with strong leadership and strategic planning abilities, driving growth and improving operations for multiple businesses. I have also recruited and built high-performing teams, consistently delivering top talent to support business objectives.

This book is not just about my journey in the staffing industry; it is also about the industry's evolution and future trends. The staffing industry has come a long way since its inception, and it continues to evolve with the changing times. The book provides insights into the staffing industry's history, from its humble beginnings to the present day, and where it is headed in the future.

The book covers a wide range of topics, including the impact of technology on staffing, the role of social media in recruiting, the importance of employer branding, and the challenges faced by recruiters. It also delves into the changing dynamics of the job market and the growing demand for skilled workers. The book provides insights into how recruiters can adapt to these changes and stay ahead of the curve.

One of the key themes of the book is the importance of gaining knowledge and the role that reading books can play in achieving success. As a child, I developed a passion for reading books, which was instilled in me by my grandfather, who was not just a doctor but also a banker. He inspired me to read and learn about different things, and I learned the art of balancing personal and professional life from him. I strongly believe that reading books is the best way to gain knowledge and stay ahead of the curve.

This book is my way of giving back to the staffing industry and sharing my experiences and insights with others. I hope that it will be a valuable resource for anyone interested in the staffing industry, whether you are a recruiter, a hiring manager, or a job seeker.

In conclusion, I would like to thank all the people who have supported me throughout my journey in the staffing industry, especially my family, friends, and colleagues. I would also like to thank the readers of this book for taking the time to read it. I hope that it will be a valuable resource for you, and I look forward to hearing your feedback.

ONE

THE EVOLUTION FROM THE EARLY DAYS TO THE PRESENT DAY.

> *"The future belongs to those who learn more skills and combine them in creative ways." -Robert Greene*

The staffing and recruiting industry has a long and fascinating history, with its roots dating back to the early 1940s. Over the years, the industry has undergone many changes and transformations, adapting to changing labor markets, technological advancements, and global economic shifts.

In this book, we will explore the evolution of staffing and recruiting, from its early days to the present day. We will examine the various factors that have shaped the industry and look at how it has responded to the changing needs of businesses and job seekers.

Early Days of Staffing and Recruiting

The use of temporary workers to fill short-term labor gaps has been around for centuries. However, it wasn't until the 1940s that the concept of temporary staffing agencies really began to take shape. During World War II, many businesses had to adjust to labor shortages and relied on temporary staffing agencies to provide workers when needed.

These early staffing agencies primarily provided clerical and administrative workers to businesses. They would hire workers and then lease them out to companies for a fee. The workers were typically paid a low wage, while the staffing agencies made a profit from the difference between the wage paid to the worker and the fee charged to the client company.

In the post-war years, the use of temporary staffing agencies continued to grow, as businesses sought flexible and cost-effective staffing solutions. However, the industry was still relatively small and primarily focused on providing temporary workers for clerical and administrative positions.

Growth and Consolidation in the 1980s and 1990s

The 1980s marked a turning point for the staffing and recruiting industry. As the economy began to recover from the recession of the early 1980s, many larger staffing and recruiting firms began acquiring smaller agencies. This trend continued into the 1990s, as the industry saw significant growth and consolidation.

During this time, the industry expanded to include a wide range of services beyond just temporary staffing. Permanent placement services, which help businesses find and hire full-time employees, became a major part of the industry. Many staffing and recruiting firms also began offering recruitment process outsourcing (RPO) services, which involve outsourcing a company's recruitment processes to an external provider.

In addition, managed services programs (MSPs) became popular in the 1990s. MSPs provide a range of services to help companies manage their contingent workforce, including temporary workers, contractors, and freelancers.

The Turn of the Century and the Impact of Technology

The turn of the century brought about significant changes to the staffing and recruiting industry, as advances in technology and globalization had a major impact on the way staffing and recruiting firms operated.

The rise of the internet and online job boards made it easier for candidates to find and apply for jobs. This made the recruitment process more efficient and streamlined, allowing staffing and recruiting firms to reach a wider pool of candidates. Job seekers could now easily access job postings from their computer or mobile device, allowing them to apply to jobs from anywhere at any time.

Globalization also had a significant impact on the staffing and recruiting industry. As businesses expanded into new markets, they needed access to local talent. Staffing and recruiting firms were able to fill this need by providing talent to companies around the world.

In recent years, the industry has continued to evolve, with a focus on innovation and the use of technology to streamline recruitment processes. Many staffing and recruiting firms now use artificial intelligence (AI) and other advanced technologies to identify and assess candidates, as well as to match them with job openings.

The Use of Artificial Intelligence (AI) and Machine Learning

One of the most significant trends in the staffing and recruiting industry in recent years has been the use of AI and machine learning to improve the recruitment process. AI can be used to scan resumes and job applications to identify top candidates, while machine learning algorithms can be used to match candidates with job openings based on their skills, experience, and other factors.

AI can also be used to conduct initial candidate screenings and assessments, saving time for recruiters and allowing them to focus on more complex tasks such as interviewing and candidate engagement. In addition, AI-powered chatbots and virtual assistants can be used to communicate with candidates and answer common questions, providing a more personalized and efficient recruitment experience.

However, the use of AI in the staffing and recruiting industry is not without its challenges. Critics have raised concerns about potential biases in AI algorithms, as well as the potential for AI to replace human recruiters altogether. It is important for staffing and recruiting firms to carefully consider these issues and ensure that their use of AI is ethical and responsible.

The Impact of the Gig Economy

Another major trend in the staffing and recruiting industry has been the rise of the gig economy. The gig economy refers to the growing trend of workers taking on short-term or freelance work rather than traditional full-time employment.

As more workers embrace the gig economy, staffing and recruiting firms have had to adapt their services to meet the needs of these workers and the companies that hire them. Many firms now offer services specifically geared toward the gig economy, such as staffing for short-term projects and freelancers.

The gig economy has also led to the rise of online platforms that connect freelancers with businesses in need of their services. These platforms, such as Upwork and Fiverr, have disrupted the traditional staffing and recruiting industry by allowing businesses to bypass staffing firms altogether and directly hire freelancers for their projects.

The COVID-19 Pandemic and the Future of Staffing and Recruiting

The COVID-19 pandemic has had a significant impact on the staffing and recruiting industry, as businesses have had to rapidly adapt to a rapidly changing labor market. Many companies have had to furlough or lay off workers, while others have seen a surge in demand for essential workers such as healthcare professionals and grocery store employees.

The pandemic has also accelerated the trend toward remote work, as many companies have shifted to remote work arrangements in order to comply with social distancing guidelines. This has led to increased demand for virtual recruitment and onboarding services, as well as for workers with the skills and experience necessary to thrive in a remote work environment.

Looking to the future, the staffing and recruiting industry is likely to continue to evolve and adapt to changing labor markets and technological advancements. The use of AI and machine learning is likely to become even more prevalent, while the gig economy is likely to continue to grow and disrupt the traditional staffing and recruiting industry.

Overall, the staffing and recruiting industry has come a long way since its early days in the 1940s. From providing temporary clerical workers to offering a wide range of services including permanent placement, RPO, and MSPs, the industry has continued to adapt and innovate in response to changing market demands. As we look toward the future, it will be interesting to see how the industry continues to evolve and shape the future of work.

Conclusion:

In conclusion, staffing and recruiting have come a long way since their early days. From traditional recruitment methods to the use of technology, the recruitment process has evolved significantly. The emergence of technology has made the recruitment process more efficient, faster, and more accurate. However, technology has also brought its own set of challenges, such as the volume of resumes and applications, high turnover rates, and concerns about bias.

Organizations that embrace technology and use it to streamline their recruitment process are likely to be more successful in attracting and retaining top talent. However, it is essential to keep in mind that technology should be used as a tool to support recruitment, not replace it entirely. The recruitment process still requires a human touch, and recruiters must build relationships with candidates to find the best fit for the organization.

As we move forward, it is likely that technology will continue to play an increasingly significant role in staffing and recruiting. Organizations that stay up to date with the latest trends and developments in technology are likely to have a competitive advantage in the recruitment process.

TWO

THE ROLE OF TECHNOLOGY IN RECRUITING

> *"The role of technology in staffing and recruiting is to streamline processes and free up time for recruiters to focus on building relationships with candidates and making strategic decisions." Alex Hattingh, Chief People Officer at Employment Hero*

Technology has transformed many aspects of human life, and the world of work is no exception. One area where technology has had a significant impact is staffing, where it has enabled organizations to streamline their hiring processes, improve candidate selection, and enhance employee retention. This essay explores the role of technology in staffing, examining its impact on recruitment, selection, and retention.

Recruitment

Recruitment is the process of identifying and attracting potential candidates for a job opening. Traditionally, recruitment has been a time-consuming and expensive process that involves advertising, reviewing resumes, conducting interviews, and checking references. However, technology has made it easier and more cost-effective to recruit candidates.

One of the most significant impacts of technology on recruitment is the use of job search websites and social media platforms to advertise job openings. Sites such as LinkedIn, Indeed, and Glassdoor allow employers to post job openings and connect with potential candidates directly. Social media platforms such as Facebook, Twitter, and Instagram also allow organizations to reach a wider audience with their job postings.

Another way technology has improved recruitment is through the use of applicant tracking systems (ATS). ATS is software that automates the recruitment process, from job posting to resume screening to interview scheduling. ATS makes it easier for recruiters to manage large volumes of resumes and identify qualified candidates quickly.

Finally, technology has made it easier for recruiters to conduct remote interviews. With the rise of video conferencing software such as Zoom and Skype, recruiters can now interview candidates from anywhere in the world without the need for in-person meetings. This has not only saved time and money but has also enabled organizations to reach a more diverse pool of candidates.

Selection

Selection is the process of evaluating candidates to determine their suitability for a job opening. Traditionally, selection has been based on resumes, interviews, and references. However, technology has enabled organizations to use more sophisticated methods of candidate selection.

One of the most significant impacts of technology on selection is the use of pre-employment assessments. Pre-employment assessments are tests that evaluate a candidate's skills, abilities, and personality traits. These assessments can include cognitive tests, behavioral tests, and situational judgment tests. Pre-employment assessments provide organizations with more objective data about candidates and help them identify the most qualified candidates for a job.

Another way technology has improved selection is through the use of artificial intelligence (AI) and machine learning. AI and machine learning algorithms can analyze large volumes of data to identify patterns and trends that may not be apparent to human recruiters. For example, AI algorithms can analyze resumes and identify candidates who are likely to be a good fit for a job based on their education, work experience, and skills.

Finally, technology has made it easier for organizations to conduct background checks on candidates. With the rise of online databases and public records, organizations can now conduct more thorough background checks on candidates quickly and easily. This has enabled organizations to identify candidates who may have criminal records, falsified their resumes, or have other issues that may disqualify them from a job.

Retention

Retention is the process of keeping employees engaged and motivated to stay with an organization. Retention is critical for organizations as it reduces turnover, improves productivity, and saves costs associated with recruiting and training new employees. Technology has had a significant impact on retention by enabling organizations to provide better training, feedback, and career development opportunities to their employees.

One of the most significant impacts of technology on retention is the use of online learning platforms. Online learning platforms such as Udemy, Coursera, and LinkedIn Learning enable organizations to provide their employees with on-demand access to training and development resources. This not only helps employees develop new skills but also demonstrates that the organization is invested in their career growth.

Another way technology has improved retention is through the use of employee feedback platforms. Employee feedback platforms such as TINYpulse and Qualtrics enable organizations to collect feedback from their employees on a regular basis. This feedback can be used to identify areas where the organization can improve, such as work-life balance, communication, and career development. By addressing these issues, organizations can create a more positive work environment that encourages employee engagement and retention.

Finally, technology has made it easier for organizations to provide flexible work arrangements to their employees. With the rise of remote work and flexible schedules, employees can now work from anywhere and at any time. This not only improves work-life balance but also allows organizations to attract and retain employees who may not be able to work in a traditional office environment.

Opportunities of Technology in Staffing and Recruiting

1. Increased Efficiency

Technology has enabled staffing and recruiting firms to automate many manual processes, such as resume screening and scheduling interviews. Automation has resulted in increased efficiency and faster turnaround times for clients and candidates. For instance, applicant tracking systems can quickly sift through resumes, sort them based on various criteria, and shortlist the most suitable candidates. This automation not only saves time but also increases the accuracy of the selection process.

Similarly, technology has enabled staffing and recruiting firms to automate interview scheduling, reducing the need for manual intervention. Tools such as calendar integrations, automatic email reminders, and follow-up notifications make the scheduling process smoother and faster, freeing up recruiters' time to focus on other important tasks.

2. Wider Reach

Technology has made it easier for staffing and recruiting firms to reach a wider pool of candidates, including those who are not actively looking for a job. Online job boards and social media platforms have enabled firms to advertise job openings to a broader audience, increasing the chances of finding highly qualified candidates.

Moreover, the use of social media platforms, such as LinkedIn and Twitter, has made it easier for staffing and recruiting firms to reach out to candidates proactively. Recruiters can search for potential candidates based on their skill sets, work history, and interests, and reach out to them with relevant job opportunities.

Additionally, technology has enabled firms to target job ads based on specific criteria such as location, experience, and education level, making it easier to reach the right candidates.

Improved Candidate Experience

Technology has enabled staffing and recruiting firms to provide a more personalized and streamlined candidate experience. Automation has made it possible to keep candidates informed about their status in the hiring process, reducing the anxiety associated with waiting for feedback.

For example, firms can use automated communication systems to keep candidates updated about their application status, interview schedules, and other relevant information. This reduces the need for manual communication and ensures that candidates are informed in a timely and efficient manner.

Furthermore, video interviews have become increasingly popular, especially in the wake of the COVID-19 pandemic, as they offer a safe and convenient alternative to in-person interviews. Video interviews save candidates time and expense, as they eliminate the need for travel, and provide a more flexible and efficient recruitment experience.

1. **Data Analytics**

Technology has made it easier for staffing and recruiting firms to collect and analyze data about job openings, candidates, and hiring trends. Analytics tools can help firms identify patterns, track metrics, and gain insights into their recruitment strategies' effectiveness.

For instance, firms can analyze data on the job openings they have advertised, the number of applications received, the quality of candidates, and the recruitment process's duration. By identifying patterns in the data, firms can improve their recruitment processes and make data-driven decisions.

Data analytics can also help firms identify areas of improvement in their diversity and inclusion efforts. For example, by analyzing the demographics of the candidate pool, firms can determine if there are any groups underrepresented in their recruitment efforts and take steps to address the imbalance.

2. **Artificial Intelligence**

Artificial intelligence (AI) has the potential to transform the staffing and recruiting industry by enabling firms to automate many tasks and make more accurate candidate matches. AI-powered chatbots and virtual assistants can help firms interact with candidates and answer their questions 24/7, reducing the workload on human recruiters. Chatbots can also assist in the screening process by asking candidates relevant questions, collecting their answers, and assessing their fit for the role.

Moreover, AI-powered tools can analyze candidate resumes and applications to identify key skills and qualifications, and rank candidates based on their suitability for the role. This automation can save time and improve the accuracy of the selection process.

Challenges of Technology in Staffing and Recruiting

1. **Reliance on Technology**

While technology has many advantages, firms must be careful not to rely too heavily on it. Over-reliance on technology can lead to a lack of personalization and human interaction, which is crucial in the staffing and recruiting industry.

For instance, automated communication systems can make the recruitment process more efficient, but they may also create a sense of impersonality, making candidates feel undervalued. Therefore, firms must balance the use of technology with human interaction to provide a personalized and positive candidate experience.

2. **Bias and Discrimination**

The use of technology in staffing and recruiting can inadvertently perpetuate biases and discrimination, especially in AI-powered systems. For instance, AI algorithms can learn to favor certain candidates based on factors such as gender, race, or education level, leading to discriminatory hiring practices.

Moreover, AI algorithms can reflect the biases inherent in the data they are trained on. If the training data includes biases, the AI system can learn and replicate those biases, perpetuating discrimination and limiting diversity in the workforce.

Therefore, firms must ensure that their recruitment processes are designed to mitigate biases and promote diversity and inclusion. This can involve using diverse recruitment teams, removing unnecessary qualifications, and monitoring and auditing their recruitment processes regularly.

3. **Security and Privacy**

The use of technology in staffing and recruiting can also raise concerns around data security and privacy. Recruitment processes involve the collection and storage of sensitive personal data, such as resumes, identification documents, and employment history.

Firms must take appropriate measures to ensure the security and privacy of this data, such as implementing data encryption, secure data storage, and access controls. They must also comply with data protection laws and regulations, such as the General Data Protection Regulation (GDPR) in the European Union and the California Consumer Privacy Act (CCPA) in the United States.

4. **Skills and Training**

The adoption of technology in staffing and recruiting requires specialized skills and training for recruiters and other staff members. Firms must invest in training and upskilling their employees to ensure they have the necessary skills to use technology effectively.

Moreover, the rapid pace of technological change means that firms must continuously adapt and update their skills and knowledge to keep up with the latest trends and best practices.

Best Practices for Leveraging Technology in Staffing and Recruiting

1. **Adopt a Human-Cantered Approach**

Firms must ensure that the use of technology in staffing and recruiting is focused on enhancing the candidate experience and facilitating human interaction, rather than replacing it. The use of technology should complement and support human efforts, rather than replace them entirely.

Therefore, firms must design their recruitment processes with a human-centered approach, placing the candidate at the center of the process. This can involve providing personalized communication, timely feedback, and a transparent and fair selection process.

2. **Invest in Quality Data**

The effectiveness of technology in staffing and recruiting is highly dependent on the quality of data used to train and power the systems. Therefore, firms must invest in collecting and maintaining high-quality data that is representative of their workforce and candidate pool.

Moreover, firms must regularly audit and monitor their data to ensure that it is accurate, up-to-date, and free from bias. This can involve implementing data validation and cleansing tools and involving diverse stakeholders in the data collection and validation process.

3. **Mitigate Bias and Discrimination**

Firms must take proactive steps to mitigate bias and discrimination in their recruitment processes when leveraging technology. This can involve using diverse recruitment teams, removing unnecessary qualifications, and monitoring and auditing their recruitment processes regularly.

Moreover, firms must ensure that the algorithms used in their AI systems are transparent and explainable, enabling them to identify and address any biases or errors in the decision-making process.

4. **Ensure Data Security and Privacy**

Firms must prioritize the security and privacy of candidate data when using technology in staffing and recruiting. This can involve implementing secure data storage and access controls, data encryption, and complying with relevant data protection laws and regulations.

Moreover, firms must ensure that their employees are trained on data security and privacy best practices, such as password management, data handling, and secure communication.

5. **Measure and Monitor Performance**

The use of technology in staffing and recruiting provides firms with a wealth of data and metrics to measure their performance and identify areas for improvement. Therefore, firms must regularly monitor and analyze their recruitment processes to identify and address any inefficiencies or areas for improvement.

Moreover, firms must use data-driven insights to continuously improve their recruitment processes, such as adjusting their selection criteria or using targeted communication to attract diverse candidates.

Conclusion

The role of technology in staffing and recruiting has significantly transformed the industry, enabling firms to automate and streamline many aspects of the recruitment process, and improving the candidate experience. However, the adoption of technology also presents significant challenges, such as bias and discrimination, security and privacy concerns, and the need for specialized skills and training.

Therefore, firms must adopt a human-centered approach to technology adoption, prioritize data quality and security, mitigate bias and discrimination, and continuously monitor and improve their recruitment processes. By leveraging technology effectively and responsibly, firms can improve the efficiency and effectiveness of their recruitment processes, and build a more diverse and inclusive workforce.

THREE

BEST PRACTICES FOR ATTRACTING AND RETAINING TOP TALENT

> *"The key to success is not just attracting top talent, but keeping them engaged, challenged, and motivated." - Sheryl Sandberg, COO of Facebook*

Attracting and retaining top talent is crucial for the success of any organization. In today's competitive business landscape, finding and keeping the best employees is more challenging than ever. To stay ahead of the competition, companies must adopt best practices for attracting and retaining top talent. In this chapter, we will explore some of the strategies that organizations can use to attract and retain the best talent.

1. **Building a strong employer brand:**

One of the most critical factors in attracting and retaining top talent is having a strong employer brand. A strong employer brand not only attracts top talent but also helps to retain existing employees. A good employer brand is built on a company's values, culture, and reputation. Organizations should focus on building a brand that resonates with their target audience and showcases their unique selling proposition.

2. **Offering competitive compensation:**

Competitive compensation is a key factor in attracting and retaining top talent. Organizations should ensure that their compensation packages are in line with industry standards and reflect the skills and experience of their employees. Offering competitive salaries, bonuses, and benefits can help to attract and retain the best employees.

3. **Providing opportunities for growth and development:**

Top talent is always looking for opportunities to grow and develop professionally. Organizations that provide their employees with opportunities for growth and development are more likely to attract and retain the best talent. Providing training programs, mentorship, and career development opportunities can help to keep employees engaged and motivated.

4. **Creating a positive work culture:**

A positive work culture is essential for attracting and retaining top talent. A positive work culture is one where employees feel valued, supported, and respected. Organizations should focus on creating a work environment where employees feel comfortable and supported. This can be achieved by promoting a healthy work-life balance, providing flexible work arrangements, and promoting open communication.

5. **Hiring the right people:**

Hiring the right people is essential for attracting and retaining top talent. Organizations should focus on hiring candidates who are a good fit for the company's culture and values. This can be achieved by using behavioral interviewing techniques and assessing candidates' cultural fit during the hiring process.

6. **Offering a supportive work environment:**

A supportive work environment is essential for retaining top talent. Organizations should provide their employees with the support they need to succeed in their roles. This can be achieved by providing employees with the resources and tools they need to perform their jobs effectively.

7. **Providing work-life balance:**

Providing work-life balance is essential for attracting and retaining top talent. Employees who have a healthy work-life balance are more productive and engaged in their work. Organizations should focus on promoting work-life balance by offering flexible work arrangements and promoting a culture of work-life balance.

8. **Creating a diverse and inclusive workplace:**

Creating a diverse and inclusive workplace is essential for attracting and retaining top talent. A diverse and inclusive workplace is one where employees feel valued and respected, regardless of their gender, race, or background. Organizations should focus on creating a culture of diversity and inclusion by promoting diversity and inclusion initiatives and creating a safe and inclusive work environment.

9. **Encouraging employee engagement:**

Encouraging employee engagement is essential for retaining top talent. Organizations should focus on creating a culture of engagement by encouraging employees to share their ideas and opinions, recognizing employee achievements, and providing regular feedback.

10. **Providing a clear career path:**

Providing a clear career path is essential for retaining top talent. Employees who see a clear path for their career are more likely to stay with an organization. Organizations should focus on providing employees with a clear career path by creating a career development plan, providing regular feedback, and offering training and development opportunities.

Conclusion:

Attracting and retaining top talent is essential for the success of any organization. Organizations that adopt best practices for attracting and retaining top talent are more likely to be successful in today's competitive business landscape.

FOUR
THE ART OF SUCCESSFUL INTERVIEWING

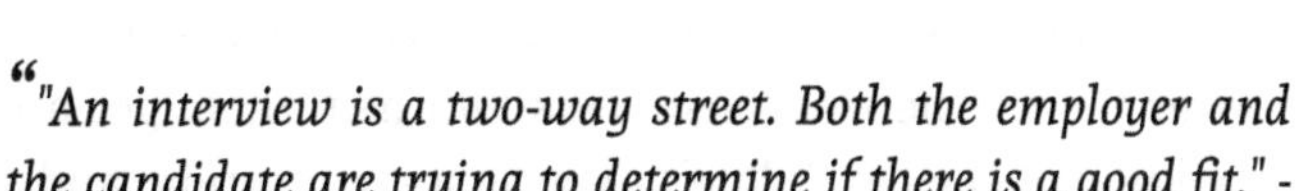

> *"An interview is a two-way street. Both the employer and the candidate are trying to determine if there is a good fit." - Alison Green*

Hiring the right candidate for a job is a crucial task for any organization. A successful interview process is essential to find the perfect fit for a position. Hiring managers play a significant role in this process as they are responsible for conducting interviews and selecting the most suitable candidate for the job. However, conducting a successful interview is not an easy task. It requires proper planning, preparation, and execution. In this chapter, we will discuss some tips and techniques that hiring managers can use to conduct successful interviews and hire the best candidates.

1. **Define the Job Requirements:**

The first step in conducting a successful interview is to define the job requirements. Hiring managers should have a clear understanding of the job responsibilities, required skills, and qualifications. This will help them create a job description that accurately reflects the job requirements. The job description should be detailed and specific, highlighting the essential skills and experience needed for the job. This will ensure that the right candidates apply for the position.

2. **Prepare for the Interview:**

Preparation is key to conducting a successful interview. Hiring managers should prepare a list of questions that they will ask the candidates during the interview. The questions should be open-ended, allowing the candidate to elaborate on their answers. The questions should also be job-specific, focusing on the candidate's relevant experience and skills.

Hiring managers should also review the candidate's resume and cover letter before the interview. This will help them get a better understanding of the candidate's experience, education, and skills. It will also help them identify any gaps in the candidate's qualifications, which they can address during the interview.

3. **Create a Comfortable Environment:**

Creating a comfortable environment is essential to putting the candidate at ease during the interview. Hiring managers should greet the candidate warmly and introduce themselves. They should also explain the interview process and how long it will take. This will help the candidate feel more relaxed and confident during the interview.

Hiring managers should also make sure that the interview room is comfortable and quiet. They should ensure that the temperature is comfortable, and there are no distractions, such as noise or interruptions.

4. **Use Behavioral Interview Techniques:**

Behavioral interview techniques are a great way to assess a candidate's skills and experience. This technique involves asking the candidate to provide specific examples of how they have demonstrated certain skills in the past. For example, a hiring manager may ask a candidate to describe a time when they had to solve a complex problem. The candidate's response will provide insight into their problem-solving skills and how they approach difficult situations.

5. **Listen Carefully:**

Listening carefully is crucial during an interview. Hiring managers should listen to the candidate's responses carefully and ask follow-up questions to clarify their answers. They should also pay attention to the candidate's body language and nonverbal cues. This can provide valuable insight into the candidate's personality, communication skills, and level of confidence.

6. **Avoid Biases:**

Hiring managers should avoid biases during the interview process. Biases can lead to discriminatory hiring practices and result in the wrong candidate being hired for the job. To avoid biases, hiring managers should focus on the candidate's skills, experience, and qualifications. They should avoid asking questions that could be seen as discriminatory, such as questions about age, gender, religion, or marital status.

7. **Use Assessment Tools:**

Assessment tools can be used to evaluate a candidate's skills and personality traits. These tools can provide valuable insights into the candidate's strengths and weaknesses. For example, a personality assessment tool can help determine if a candidate is a good fit for the company's culture.

Hiring managers should use assessment tools as a supplement to the interview process. They should not rely solely on the results of the assessment tools to make hiring decisions.

8. **Provide Feedback:**

During the interview process, it is important for hiring managers to provide feedback to the candidate. This helps the candidate understand how they performed during the interview and what they can improve on for future interviews.

Feedback can also be beneficial to the hiring manager as it can help them improve their interview skills. By providing feedback to candidates, hiring managers can identify areas where they can improve their interview techniques and communication skills.

When providing feedback to candidates, hiring managers should be specific and constructive. They should focus on the candidate's strengths and weaknesses, and provide examples of how they can improve. For example, if a candidate struggled with answering a particular question, the hiring manager can provide tips on how to approach that type of question in the future.

It is also important for hiring managers to provide feedback in a timely manner. Candidates are often anxious to hear back after an interview, and delays in providing feedback can lead to frustration and anxiety.

9. **Use Technology:**

Technology can be a valuable tool for hiring managers. It can streamline the interview process, making it more efficient and effective. Video conferencing tools, such as Zoom or Skype, can be used for remote interviews, allowing hiring managers to interview candidates who are not in the same location.

Applicant tracking systems (ATS) can also be used to manage the interview process. ATS systems can help hiring managers keep track of resumes, schedule interviews, and manage candidate communications.

10. **Follow Up:**

Following up with candidates after an interview is important. It shows that the company is interested in the candidate and values their time. Hiring managers should follow up with candidates promptly, thanking them for their time and reiterating the next steps in the hiring process.

If the candidate is not selected for the job, it is important to provide feedback and let them know why they were not selected. This can help the candidate improve their skills and prepare better for future interviews.

Conclusion:

Conducting a successful interview is crucial to hiring the right candidate for a job. Hiring managers play a significant role in this process, and their skills and techniques can make a significant impact on the success of the interview process. By following these tips and techniques, hiring managers can improve their interview skills, hire the best candidates, and build a successful team.

FIVE
DIVERSITY AND INCLUSION IN STAFFING AND RECRUITING

> *"Diversity is about all of us, and about us having to figure out how to walk through this world together." - Jacqueline Woodson*

Diversity and inclusion are important concepts in staffing and recruiting. Diversity refers to the differences that exist among people, including race, ethnicity, gender, age, religion, sexual orientation, and physical abilities. Inclusion, on the other hand, refers to creating an environment where everyone feels valued, respected, and included. Inclusion is about creating an environment where everyone can contribute their unique skills and experiences to the organization.

There are many challenges that organizations face when it comes to diversity and inclusion in staffing and recruiting. These challenges include unconscious bias, lack of diversity in the applicant pool, and a lack of commitment to diversity and inclusion from leadership. In this paper, we will explore these challenges and offer solutions for creating a more diverse and inclusive workforce.

Challenges:

Unconscious Bias

One of the biggest challenges in diversity and inclusion in staffing and recruiting is unconscious bias. Unconscious bias is the implicit, often unintentional, attitudes and beliefs that influence our decisions and actions. Everyone has unconscious biases, and they can impact our decision-making in ways that we are not aware of.

For example, a hiring manager may unconsciously favor candidates who are similar to them in terms of race, gender, or educational background. This can lead to a lack of diversity in the workforce, as candidates who are different from the hiring manager may be overlooked.

Lack of Diversity in the Applicant Pool

Another challenge in diversity and inclusion in staffing and recruiting is the lack of diversity in the applicant pool. This can be due to a variety of reasons, including a lack of outreach to diverse communities, a lack of diversity in the industry, and systemic barriers that prevent certain groups from pursuing certain careers.

For example, women and minorities may be underrepresented in certain industries due to historic discrimination and lack of opportunities. This can result in a lack of diversity in the applicant pool, which can make it difficult for organizations to create a diverse and inclusive workforce.

Lack of Commitment to Diversity and Inclusion from Leadership

Finally, a lack of commitment to diversity and inclusion from leadership can be a significant challenge in staffing and recruiting. Without a commitment from leadership, diversity and inclusion initiatives may not be given the necessary resources or support to be successful. Additionally, without a commitment from leadership, employees may not feel empowered to speak up about issues related to diversity and inclusion.

Solutions:

Unconscious Bias Training

One solution to the challenge of unconscious bias is unconscious bias training. Unconscious bias training is designed to help individuals recognize their own unconscious biases and learn strategies for mitigating their impact. This can include techniques for challenging assumptions, seeking out diverse perspectives, and recognizing the importance of diversity in decision-making.

Unconscious bias training can be particularly effective when it is integrated into the hiring process. For example, hiring managers can be trained to recognize their biases and to use structured interviews and objective criteria to evaluate candidates. This can help to ensure that all candidates are evaluated fairly and that the best candidate is selected, regardless of their race, gender, or other factors.

Diversity Outreach and Recruitment

Another solution to the challenge of a lack of diversity in the applicant pool is diversity outreach and recruitment. This can include targeted outreach to diverse communities, partnerships with community organizations, and targeted recruitment efforts.

For example, an organization may partner with a local community organization to host a job fair that is targeted towards diverse candidates. This can help to increase the number of diverse candidates in the applicant pool and can also help to create connections between the organization and the community.

In addition, organizations can use targeted recruitment efforts to reach out to diverse candidates. This can include advertising in publications or websites that are targeted towards diverse candidates, attending career fairs that are focused on diversity, or reaching out to diversity-focused professional organizations.

Leadership Commitment and Accountability

challenge of a lack of commitment to diversity and inclusion from leadership is a strong commitment and accountability from the top of the organization. This can include setting diversity and inclusion goals, regularly measuring progress towards those goals, and holding leadership accountable for meeting those goals.

For example, an organization may set a goal of increasing the representation of women and minorities in leadership positions by a certain percentage within a specific timeframe. This goal can be communicated to all employees and progress towards the goal can be regularly tracked and reported to leadership.

Additionally, leadership can be held accountable for meeting these goals through performance evaluations and other forms of accountability. This can help to ensure that diversity and inclusion are prioritized throughout the organization and that progress towards these goals is being made.

Conclusion

Diversity and inclusion are important concepts in staffing and recruiting. However, there are many challenges that organizations face in creating a diverse and inclusive workforce. These challenges include unconscious bias, a lack of diversity in the applicant pool, and a lack of commitment to diversity and inclusion from leadership.

There are solutions to these challenges, including unconscious bias training, diversity outreach and recruitment, and leadership commitment and accountability. By implementing these solutions, organizations can create a more diverse and inclusive workforce, which can lead to a variety of benefits, including increased creativity, innovation, and productivity. Ultimately, creating a diverse and inclusive workforce is not only the right thing to do, but it is also good for business.

SIX

NAVIGATING LEGAL AND COMPLIANCE ISSUES IN STAFFING AND RECRUITING

> *"Compliance is not just about avoiding legal risks, it's also about doing the right thing for your employees, clients, and the community." – Unknown*

The staffing and recruiting industry is a complex and highly regulated field. HR professionals involved in staffing and recruiting must navigate a variety of legal and compliance issues, including anti-discrimination laws, labor laws, background checks, and employment contracts. Failing to comply with these laws and regulations can lead to costly lawsuits, penalties, and reputational damage.

This guide is designed to help HR professionals navigate the legal and compliance issues in staffing and recruiting. We will cover the key laws and regulations that apply to staffing and recruiting, and provide practical guidance on how to comply with them.

Anti-Discrimination Laws

Anti-discrimination laws are a critical area of concern for HR professionals involved in staffing and recruiting. These laws prohibit discrimination based on a variety of protected characteristics, including race, gender, age, religion, national origin, and disability.

The primary federal law governing anti-discrimination in the workplace is Title VII of the Civil Rights Act of 1964. Title VII prohibits discrimination based on race, color, religion, sex, and national origin. In addition to Title VII, there are a variety of other federal and state laws that prohibit discrimination based on other protected characteristics.

To comply with anti-discrimination laws, HR professionals should ensure that their hiring practices do not discriminate against candidates based on their protected characteristics. This includes reviewing job descriptions and requirements to ensure they are job-related and do not have a disparate impact on protected groups. HR professionals should also ensure that all job postings and advertisements comply with anti-discrimination laws and avoid using language that could be interpreted as discriminatory.

In addition to avoiding discrimination in hiring, HR professionals should also ensure that their company's policies and practices do not discriminate against employees based on their protected characteristics. This includes providing reasonable accommodations for employees with disabilities and ensuring that all employees are treated fairly and equally regardless of their protected characteristics.

Labor Laws

HR professionals involved in staffing and recruiting must also navigate a variety of labor laws. These laws govern the relationship between employers and employees and include regulations related to minimum wage, overtime pay, and child labor.

The primary federal law governing labor laws is the Fair Labor Standards Act (FLSA). The FLSA establishes minimum wage and overtime pay requirements, as well as regulations related to child labor. In addition to the FLSA, there are a variety of other federal and state labor laws that HR professionals must comply with.

To comply with labor laws, HR professionals should ensure that all employees are classified correctly as either exempt or non-exempt. Exempt employees are typically salaried and not eligible for overtime pay, while non-exempt employees are typically hourly and eligible for overtime pay. HR professionals should also ensure that all employees are paid at least the minimum wage and receive overtime pay if they work more than 40 hours per week.

Background Checks

Background checks are a common practice in staffing and recruiting, but they must be conducted in compliance with applicable laws and regulations. The primary federal law governing background checks is the Fair Credit Reporting Act (FCRA). The FCRA establishes requirements related to obtaining and using consumer reports, including background checks.

To comply with the FCRA, HR professionals should ensure that they obtain written consent from candidates before conducting a background check. They should also provide candidates with a copy of the report and a summary of their rights under the FCRA. HR professionals should also ensure that they only use background check information that is job-related and consistent with business necessity.

Employment Contracts

Employment contracts are another area of concern for HR professionals involved in staffing and recruiting. These contracts govern the relationship between employers and employees and can include a variety of provisions related to compensation, benefits, and termination.

To comply with employment contract laws, HR professionals should ensure that all contracts are in writing and signed by both the employer and employee. They should also ensure that all contracts comply with applicable laws and regulations, including those related to minimum wage, overtime pay, and anti-discrimination.

Employment contracts should clearly outline the terms and conditions of employment, including the employee's duties and responsibilities, compensation and benefits, and the length of the employment period. HR professionals should ensure that all contract provisions are legal and enforceable under applicable laws.

In addition to complying with laws related to employment contracts, HR professionals should also ensure that they provide all employees with required notices and disclosures, such as notices related to their rights under the Family and Medical Leave Act (FMLA) or the Affordable Care Act (ACA).

Independent Contractors

Many staffing and recruiting companies rely on independent contractors to perform work for their clients. However, misclassifying workers as independent contractors instead of employees can lead to significant legal and financial consequences.

To comply with laws related to independent contractors, HR professionals should ensure that all workers are properly classified based on the nature of their work and their level of control over their work. Factors that are used to determine whether a worker is an employee or an independent contractor include the degree of control the employer has over the worker, the worker's investment in their equipment or materials, and the degree of independence the worker has in performing their work.

HR professionals should also ensure that they comply with tax laws related to independent contractors, including filing appropriate tax forms and providing workers with required tax documents.

Data Privacy

Data privacy is another critical area of concern for HR professionals involved in staffing and recruiting. Staffing and recruiting companies collect and maintain a significant amount of sensitive information about their clients and candidates, including personal information, employment history, and criminal background.

To comply with data privacy laws, HR professionals should ensure that they have appropriate data security measures in place to protect sensitive information from unauthorized access and disclosure. This includes implementing policies and procedures related to data access, storage, and disposal.

HR professionals should also ensure that they comply with applicable data privacy laws, including the General Data Protection Regulation (GDPR) and the California Consumer Privacy Act (CCPA). These laws establish requirements related to data collection, use, and disclosure, and provide individuals with certain rights related to their personal information.

Conclusion

Navigating legal and compliance issues in staffing and recruiting can be a challenging task for HR professionals. However, by understanding and complying with applicable laws and regulations related to anti-discrimination, labor, background checks, employment contracts, independent contractors, and data privacy,

HR professionals can reduce the risk of costly lawsuits, penalties, and reputational damage.

HR professionals should work closely with legal counsel and stay up-to-date on changes to applicable laws and regulations to ensure that their company's staffing and recruiting practices are in compliance with all legal requirements. By doing so, they can protect their company's reputation and ensure that they are providing fair and equal opportunities to all candidates and employees.

SEVEN

STAFFING AND RECRUITING IN THE GIG ECONOMY

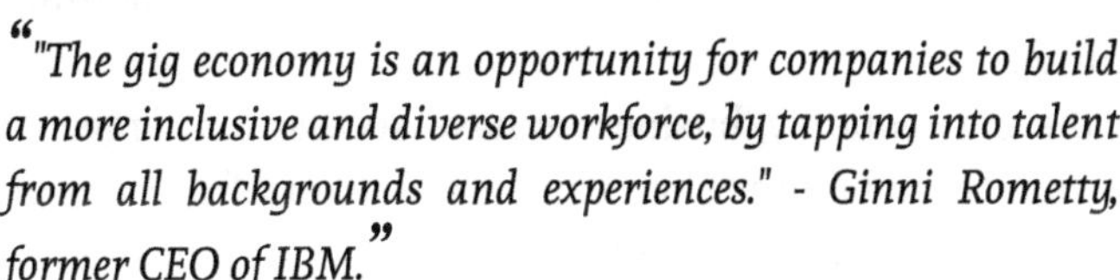

> "*"The gig economy is an opportunity for companies to build a more inclusive and diverse workforce, by tapping into talent from all backgrounds and experiences." - Ginni Rometty, former CEO of IBM.*"

The gig economy has transformed the way people work and has had a significant impact on the traditional employment model. Staffing and recruiting in the gig economy is a new phenomenon that has emerged with the rise of independent contractors, freelancers, and other non-traditional workers. This paper will discuss the impact of the gig economy on staffing and recruiting, and explore the opportunities and challenges that it presents for businesses.

The Gig Economy

The gig economy refers to the trend of people working on a freelance, temporary, or short-term basis, rather than as full-time employees. It is characterized by a workforce that is flexible, mobile, and independent. This trend has been facilitated by advances in technology, which have made it easier for people to work remotely and communicate with clients and colleagues across the globe. The gig economy has created opportunities for workers who prefer a more flexible work-life balance, and for businesses that need to scale up or down quickly in response to market demands.

Impact on Staffing and Recruiting

The gig economy has had a significant impact on staffing and recruiting. In the past, businesses relied on traditional employment models, where they hired full-time employees who worked for the company for many years. However, the gig economy has introduced a new type of worker, who is more independent and flexible. This has led to a shift in the way businesses approach staffing and recruiting.

In the gig economy, businesses have access to a larger pool of talent than ever before. They can hire workers from around the world, and can scale up or down quickly in response to market demands. This has created opportunities for businesses to tap into the skills of highly specialized workers, who may not be available in their local labor market. It has also created opportunities for workers who prefer a more flexible work-life balance, and who may not be interested in traditional employment models.

Opportunities for Businesses

The gig economy presents many opportunities for businesses. One of the most significant is the ability to tap into a larger pool of talent. Businesses can hire workers from around the world, and can access highly specialized skills that may not be available in their local labor market. This can help businesses to innovate and stay competitive, by bringing in fresh perspectives and ideas.

The gig economy also allows businesses to scale up or down quickly in response to market demands. This can help businesses to reduce costs and increase efficiency, by only hiring workers when they are needed. It can also help businesses to respond to changes in the market quickly, by adjusting their workforce as needed.

Challenges for Businesses

While the gig economy presents many opportunities for businesses, it also presents challenges. One of the biggest challenges is managing a remote workforce. In the gig economy, workers are often spread out across the globe, and may work on different schedules. This can make it difficult to manage projects and ensure that workers are meeting deadlines.

Another challenge is maintaining quality standards. In the gig economy, businesses may be working with workers who they have never met in person, and who may have different cultural or linguistic backgrounds. This can make it difficult to ensure that the work being produced meets the required standards.

Conclusion

The gig economy has transformed the way people work, and has had a significant impact on staffing and recruiting. Businesses have access to a larger pool of talent than ever before, and can scale up or down quickly in response to market demands. However, the gig economy also presents challenges, such as managing a remote workforce and maintaining quality standards. Despite these challenges, the gig economy presents many opportunities for businesses to innovate, stay competitive, and grow.

EIGHT

THE ROLE OF EMPLOYER BRANDING IN STAFFING AND RECRUITING

> *"Your employer brand is what people say about you when you're not in the room." - Jeff Bezos*

Employer branding is a strategic approach that helps an organization in attracting and retaining the best talent by creating a positive image of the company as an employer. The term "employer brand" refers to the perception of a company as an employer in the eyes of current and potential employees, as well as the general public. It is the image that a company projects to the world, which is shaped by its culture, values, policies, and practices. In today's competitive job market, employer branding plays a critical role in staffing and recruiting. This chapter will explore the importance of employer branding and the steps that organizations can take to build a strong employer brand.

Importance of Employer Branding:

The importance of employer branding in staffing and recruiting cannot be overstated. In today's talent-driven job market, it has become crucial for companies to have a strong employer brand. A positive employer brand can help a company in several ways, including:

Attracting Top Talent: A strong employer brand can help a company attract top talent by making it an employer of choice. In a competitive job market, candidates have multiple options to choose from, and a positive employer brand can make a company stand out from the crowd. A good employer brand helps in attracting the right candidates who are not only skilled and qualified but also share the company's values and culture.

Reducing Recruitment Costs: A strong employer brand can help a company reduce recruitment costs by attracting more qualified candidates. When a company has a positive reputation as an employer, it can attract more candidates through employee referrals and social media. This can reduce the need for expensive recruitment campaigns and lower recruitment costs.

Improving Retention: A strong employer brand can help a company in retaining its best employees. When employees feel that their company is a great place to work, they are more likely to stay with the company for the long term. This can lead to higher employee engagement and productivity, which can benefit the company in the long run.

Enhancing Customer Perception: A strong employer brand can also enhance the customer perception of a company. When a company has a positive reputation as an employer, it can translate into a positive perception of the company's products and services. This can help in building customer loyalty and increasing sales.

Steps to Building a Strong Employer Brand:

Building a strong employer brand requires a strategic approach that involves several steps. The following are the steps that organizations can take to build a strong employer brand:

1. **Define Your Employer Brand:**

The first step in building a strong employer brand is to define what your employer brand stands for. This involves understanding your company's culture, values, and mission and aligning them with your employer brand. You need to identify your unique selling points as an employer and what makes your company an attractive place to work. This can be achieved by conducting surveys, focus groups, and interviews with current and former employees, as well as external stakeholders.

2. **Develop Your Employee Value Proposition (EVP):**

Once you have defined your employer brand, the next step is to develop your Employee Value Proposition (EVP). Your EVP is a statement that outlines what you offer to your employees in exchange for their skills, experience, and expertise. It should highlight the benefits of working for your company and what sets you apart from your competitors. Your EVP should be communicated consistently across all channels, including your website, social media, and job advertisements.

3. **Create a Positive Candidate Experience:**

Creating a positive candidate experience is crucial in building a strong employer brand. It starts with the job application process and extends to the entire recruitment process. A positive candidate experience involves providing clear and timely communication, personalized feedback, and a transparent recruitment process. This can help in creating a positive impression of your company as an employer, even for candidates who are not ultimately selected.

4. **Engage Your Employees:**

Employee engagement is a critical factor in building a strong employer brand. Engaged employees are more likely to become brand ambassadors and promote your company as an employer of choice. They are also more likely to stay with the company for the long term, which can help in reducing recruitment costs and improving retention rates. To engage your employees, you need to create a positive work environment that fosters open communication, collaboration, and employee development. You should also provide opportunities for employee recognition, feedback, and involvement in decision-making.

5. **Leverage Social Media:**

Social media has become a powerful tool in building an employer brand. It provides a platform for companies to showcase their culture, values, and job opportunities to a wider audience. You can use social media to share employee stories, highlight company events and initiatives, and promote job vacancies. Social media also provides an opportunity for candidates and employees to engage with your company and share their experiences, which can help in building a positive employer brand.

6. **Build a Strong Corporate Social Responsibility (CSR) Program:**

A strong CSR program can also help in building a strong employer brand. CSR involves a company's commitment to social and environmental responsibility, which can enhance its reputation as a socially responsible employer. A CSR program can involve initiatives such as volunteering, charitable giving, and sustainability efforts. By communicating your CSR initiatives to your employees and external stakeholders, you can demonstrate your commitment to making a positive impact in the community and the environment.

7. **Measure and Monitor Your Employer Brand:**

Measuring and monitoring your employer brand is essential in evaluating the effectiveness of your branding efforts. You can use metrics such as employee satisfaction, employee turnover, recruitment cost, and candidate feedback to track the performance of your employer brand. You can also use online tools and social media analytics to monitor your online reputation and respond to feedback and reviews. By regularly monitoring your employer brand, you can identify areas for improvement and adjust your branding strategy accordingly.

Conclusion:

Building a strong employer brand is essential in staffing and recruiting. A positive employer brand can help in attracting top talent, reducing recruitment costs, improving retention rates, and enhancing customer perception. To build a strong employer brand, organizations need to define their employer brand, develop their EVP, create a positive candidate experience, engage their employees, leverage social media, build a strong CSR program, and measure and monitor their employer brand. By taking these steps, organizations can create a positive image of themselves as an employer of choice, which can help in attracting and retaining the best talent in the job market.

NINE

EFFECTIVE ON-BOARDING STRATEGIES

> *"Onboarding is not just about introducing new hires to the company, it's about introducing them to the company's culture and values." - Unknown"*

Onboarding is the process of integrating a new employee into an organization and familiarizing them with the company's culture, policies, and procedures. Effective onboarding is critical to the success of both the employee and the organization. It can help to reduce turnover, increase job satisfaction, and improve employee engagement. In this chapter, we will discuss effective onboarding strategies to ensure new hires hit the ground running.

1. **Start before the employee's first day**

Effective onboarding starts before the employee's first day on the job. A new employee's first impression of the company begins with their initial interactions with HR and the hiring manager.

Therefore, it is important to make sure that all the necessary paperwork is completed before the employee's first day. This includes filling out all the required forms, such as tax forms, employment agreements, and benefits enrollment forms.

It is also a good idea to provide the new hire with an employee handbook or other materials that outline the company's policies and procedures. This will allow the new employee to become familiar with the company's culture and expectations before their first day.

Finally, consider setting up an orientation meeting with the new employee's supervisor or a member of the HR team to go over the onboarding process and answer any questions the new employee may have.

2. **Create a comprehensive onboarding plan**

A comprehensive onboarding plan is critical to ensuring new hires hit the ground running. The plan should include a timeline of activities and milestones, as well as a list of the resources and tools that the new employee will need to be successful in their new role.

The onboarding plan should also include a clear outline of the new employee's responsibilities and expectations. This will help to ensure that the new hire understands what is expected of them and can begin working towards meeting those expectations from day one.

3. **Assign a buddy or mentor**

Assigning a buddy or mentor to the new employee can be an effective way to ensure they hit the ground running. A buddy or mentor can provide the new employee with guidance and support as they navigate their new role and the company culture. They can also help the new employee to build relationships with their colleagues and feel more comfortable in their new environment.

When selecting a buddy or mentor, it is important to choose someone who has experience in the same role or department as the new hire. This will allow them to provide relevant guidance and support.

4. **Provide job-specific training**

Job-specific training is essential to ensuring new hires hit the ground running. The training should be tailored to the new employee's specific role and responsibilities, and should cover all the necessary skills and knowledge they will need to be successful.

The training should be provided in a variety of formats, including in-person training sessions, online courses, and job shadowing opportunities. This will allow the new employee to learn in a variety of ways and will help to reinforce their understanding of the material.

5. **Provide opportunities for socialization**

Socialization is an important part of the onboarding process. It allows new employees to build relationships with their colleagues and feel more comfortable in their new environment. Therefore, it is important to provide opportunities for socialization during the onboarding process.

This can include team-building activities, such as group lunches or outings, as well as informal opportunities for the new employee to get to know their colleagues, such as coffee breaks or after-work events.

6. **Provide ongoing support and feedback**

Ongoing support and feedback are critical to the success of the onboarding process. It is important to check in with the new employee regularly to see how they are doing and provide any additional support they may need.

It is also important to provide feedback on the new employee's performance. This can include both positive feedback and constructive criticism. Regular feedback can help the new employee to understand their strengths and weaknesses and work towards improving their performance.

7. **Set clear goals and expectations**

Setting clear goals and expectations for the new employee is critical to ensuring they hit the ground running. This should include specific objectives for the new employee to achieve within the first few weeks or months of their employment.

Setting clear goals and expectations will help the new employee to understand what is expected of them and provide them with a clear roadmap for success. It will also help to ensure that the new employee is able to contribute to the organization from day one.

8. **Provide opportunities for professional development**

Providing opportunities for professional development is important for new employees, as it allows them to grow and develop within their role. This can include training programs, mentorship opportunities, and access to resources such as books, articles, and online courses.

Providing opportunities for professional development will also help to increase the employee's job satisfaction and engagement, which can lead to increased retention rates.

9. **Celebrate milestones**

Celebrating milestones is an important part of the onboarding process. This can include recognizing the new employee's achievements, such as completing training or achieving specific objectives.

Celebrating milestones will help to reinforce the new employee's positive behavior and encourage them to continue to work hard and achieve success within the organization.

10. **Continuously evaluate and improve the onboarding process**

Finally, it is important to continuously evaluate and improve the onboarding process. This can include soliciting feedback from new hires and their supervisors to identify areas for improvement.

Continuously evaluating and improving the onboarding process will help to ensure that it remains effective and relevant to the needs of the organization and its employees.

Conclusion

Effective onboarding is critical to the success of both the employee and the organization. It can help to reduce turnover, increase job satisfaction, and improve employee engagement. To ensure new hires hit the ground running, it is important to start before the employee's first day, create a comprehensive onboarding plan, assign a buddy or mentor, provide job-specific training, provide opportunities for socialization, provide ongoing support and feedback, set clear goals and expectations, provide opportunities for professional development, celebrate milestones, and continuously evaluate and improve the onboarding process. By following these strategies, organizations can create a positive and productive onboarding experience for new employees.

TEN

MANAGING REMOTE WORKFORCE

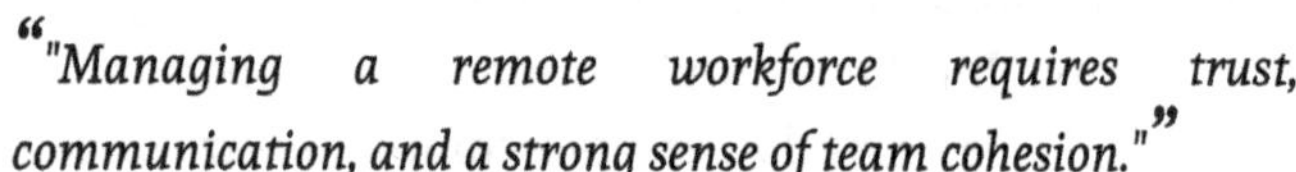

> *"Managing a remote workforce requires trust, communication, and a strong sense of team cohesion."*

Over the past few years, remote work has become increasingly popular. The COVID-19 pandemic has accelerated this trend, forcing many businesses to transition to remote work practically overnight. While remote work can offer many benefits, such as increased flexibility, it can also present unique challenges for managers. Managing remote employees requires a different approach than managing employees in a traditional office setting. In this chapter, we will explore some strategies for managing remote workforces successfully.

Communication is Key

One of the most critical elements of managing remote workforces is communication. In a traditional office setting, it is easy to pop into someone's office or have a quick chat in the break room. However, when working remotely, these opportunities for spontaneous communication are limited. Therefore, it is essential to establish clear communication channels to ensure that everyone is on the same page.

First, consider the tools you will use for communication. Email is still the most popular form of communication in the workplace, but it can be slow and inefficient. Instant messaging platforms like Slack and Microsoft Teams can provide a more efficient way to communicate. These tools allow for real-time communication, which can be especially helpful when working on a project that requires collaboration.

Video conferencing is another useful tool for remote communication. It allows you to have face-to-face conversations with your team, which can help build relationships and increase engagement. Video conferencing can also be useful for team meetings, allowing everyone to see and hear each other and participate in discussions.

It's also essential to establish clear communication expectations. Make sure your team knows when they should be available for communication and what channels they should use. It can also be helpful to establish guidelines for response times, so everyone knows what to expect.

Finally, be proactive about communication. Check in with your team regularly to see how they are doing and offer support when needed. Encourage your team to communicate with each other, as well. Building a culture of open communication can help keep everyone on the same page and prevent misunderstandings.

Set Clear Expectations

When managing a remote workforce, it's crucial to set clear expectations. In a traditional office setting, it's easy to see when someone is working and when they are not. However, when working remotely, it can be difficult to determine when someone is available and when they are not. Therefore, it's essential to establish clear expectations for when work should be done and what the goals are.

Start by setting clear goals and deadlines for your team. Make sure everyone knows what they are working toward and what their role is in achieving those goals. Set realistic deadlines, taking into account the fact that people may have other responsibilities, such as caring for children or elderly parents.

It's also important to establish clear working hours. While remote work offers more flexibility, it's essential to establish when your team is expected to be available for work. Make sure everyone knows what their working hours are and what is expected of them during that time.

Finally, be clear about what success looks like. Make sure your team knows what they need to do to be successful and how their success will be measured. Provide regular feedback to help them stay on track and adjust their approach as needed.

Build Trust

Trust is crucial when managing remote workforces. When you can't see your team working, it can be easy to assume that they are not working. Therefore, it's essential to build trust with your team to ensure that everyone is on the same page.

Start by hiring the right people. Look for candidates who are self-motivated and can work independently. These traits are essential for remote work, where there are often fewer opportunities for supervision and guidance.

Provide your team with the tools and resources they need to succeed. Make sure they have access to the software and hardware they need to do their jobs effectively. Provide training and support to help them learn how to use these tools and resources.

Be available to your team. When your team members have questions or concerns, make sure you are available to help them. Respond promptly to emails and messages, and schedule regular check-ins to provide feedback and support.

Encourage collaboration and teamwork. Remote work can be isolating, so it's essential to provide opportunities for your team to work together. Encourage them to collaborate on projects and share their ideas and expertise. Use tools like video conferencing and instant messaging to facilitate communication and collaboration.

Recognize and reward your team's efforts. When your team members do excellent work, make sure you recognize and reward them. Celebrate their successes and provide incentives for exceptional performance. This can help build a sense of camaraderie and motivate your team to continue doing their best work.

Foster a Positive Culture

Building a positive culture is essential for managing remote workforces successfully. A positive culture can help keep your team motivated and engaged, even when working remotely.

Start by promoting a healthy work-life balance. Encourage your team to take breaks and prioritize their mental and physical health. Provide resources and support for mental health and wellness, such as access to counseling or mindfulness apps.

Create opportunities for socialization and team building. Remote work can be isolating, so it's essential to provide opportunities for your team to connect socially. Schedule virtual team building activities or social events to help your team get to know each other and build relationships.

Encourage professional development. Remote work can be an excellent opportunity for your team members to learn new skills and take on new challenges. Provide opportunities for professional development, such as online training or conferences, to help your team grow and develop.

Finally, lead by example. As a manager, your behavior sets the tone for your team. Make sure you are modeling the behavior you want to see in your team members. Be positive, proactive, and responsive, and your team is likely to follow suit.

Conclusion

Managing remote workforces requires a different approach than managing employees in a traditional office setting. Communication, setting clear expectations, building trust, and fostering a positive culture are all essential elements of successful remote management. By following these strategies, you can help your team stay motivated and engaged, even when working remotely. Ultimately, a successful remote workforce is one where everyone feels supported, connected, and empowered to do their best work.

ELEVEN

THE IMPACT OF AI AND AUTOMATION ON STAFFING AND RECRUITING

> *"The impact of AI and automation on staffing and recruiting is undeniable, but with the right strategies in place, the industry can adapt and thrive in this new era of technological innovation."- Unknown*

The rise of artificial intelligence (AI) and automation technologies has revolutionized many industries, including staffing and recruiting. These technologies have transformed the way companies find, screen, and hire employees, and have enabled significant improvements in the efficiency and accuracy of the hiring process. However, as AI and automation become increasingly prevalent in the staffing and recruiting industry, they also raise important questions and challenges for companies, job seekers, and society as a whole. In this paper, we will explore the impact of AI and automation on staffing and recruiting, and discuss some of the implications and challenges that arise from these changes.

The Benefits of AI and Automation in Staffing and Recruiting

AI and automation technologies have a number of potential benefits for the staffing and recruiting industry. These technologies can help companies to identify and attract top talent more quickly and efficiently, reducing the time and resources required for the hiring process. For example, AI-powered job boards and recruitment platforms can automatically match job seekers with relevant job postings, based on their skills and experience, and can provide employers with a pool of pre-screened and qualified candidates to choose from.

AI and automation can also improve the accuracy and fairness of the hiring process, by removing human bias and subjectivity from candidate screening and selection. For example, AI-powered tools can analyze job applications and resumes, and identify candidates with the most relevant skills and experience, without being influenced by factors such as race, gender, or age. This can help to reduce discrimination in hiring, and increase diversity in the workforce.

Another benefit of AI and automation in staffing and recruiting is that these technologies can help to streamline and optimize the onboarding process, reducing the time and resources required to train new employees. For example, AI-powered training programs can provide personalized and interactive learning experiences, tailored to each employee's individual needs and learning style.

Finally, AI and automation can help to improve the overall employee experience, by enabling more effective performance management and employee engagement. For example, AI-powered performance management tools can provide real-time feedback and coaching to employees, helping them to improve their skills and achieve their goals more quickly and effectively.

The Challenges and Implications of AI and Automation in Staffing and Recruiting

While AI and automation have many potential benefits for the staffing and recruiting industry, they also raise important questions and challenges for companies, job seekers, and society as a whole. Some of the key challenges and implications of AI and automation in staffing and recruiting include:

Ethical and Legal Concerns

One of the primary concerns with AI and automation in staffing and recruiting is the potential for bias and discrimination. While AI and automation can help to remove human bias from the hiring process, they can also introduce their own biases and limitations, based on the data and algorithms used to train them. For example, if AI tools are trained on data sets that are skewed towards a particular demographic group, they may be less effective at identifying and attracting diverse candidates.

This raises important ethical and legal questions about the use of AI and automation in hiring. Companies must ensure that their AI and automation tools are designed and implemented in a way that is fair, unbiased, and compliant with applicable laws and regulations.

Skills and Training Requirements

Another challenge with AI and automation in staffing and recruiting is the need for new skills and training requirements. As AI and automation technologies become more prevalent in the industry, companies will need to invest in training and upskilling their employees to effectively use and manage these tools. This may require significant investments in time and resources, and may also require companies to rethink their hiring and talent management strategies.

Job seekers will also need to develop new skills and competencies to succeed in an increasingly automated and AI-powered job market. This may require significant investments in education and training, and may also require individuals to be more adaptable and flexible in their career paths and job search strategies.

Changes in Job Roles and Responsibilities

The rise of AI and automation in staffing and recruiting is also likely to lead to changes in job roles and responsibilities. For example, some tasks that were previously performed by human recruiters, such as candidate screening and selection, may now be automated. This may lead to a shift in the focus of human recruiters towards more strategic and value-added activities, such as building relationships with candidates and clients, and developing talent acquisition strategies.

However, it may also lead to job displacement for some recruiters and other staffing and recruiting professionals, who may need to develop new skills and competencies in order to stay relevant in the industry.

Impact on Candidate Experience

While AI and automation have the potential to improve the efficiency and accuracy of the hiring process, they may also have an impact on the candidate experience. For example, candidates may feel that they are being evaluated solely on the basis of their skills and experience, without being given the opportunity to showcase their personality and fit with the company culture.

Additionally, AI-powered recruitment platforms may not provide candidates with the same level of human interaction and support that they would receive from a traditional recruitment process. This may lead to a less engaging and personalized candidate experience, which could negatively impact the employer brand and the company's ability to attract top talent.

Impact on Diversity and Inclusion

As mentioned earlier, one of the potential benefits of AI and automation in staffing and recruiting is the ability to remove human bias and increase diversity in the workforce. However, there is also a risk that AI and automation may perpetuate existing biases and inequalities, if they are not designed and implemented in a way that is sensitive to diversity and inclusion issues.

For example, if AI tools are trained on data sets that do not include diverse candidates, they may be less effective at identifying and attracting candidates from underrepresented groups. Additionally, if AI and automation tools are not designed to account for the unique experiences and perspectives of different candidate groups, they may inadvertently perpetuate stereotypes and biases.

Cybersecurity Risks

Finally, the increased use of AI and automation in staffing and recruiting also raises cybersecurity risks. Companies must ensure that their recruitment platforms and tools are secure and protected against cyber threats, to prevent the theft or misuse of sensitive candidate data. Additionally, companies must ensure that their AI and automation tools are designed to comply with data protection and privacy regulations, to protect candidate privacy and prevent unauthorized access or use of personal data.

Conclusion

In conclusion, the rise of AI and automation in staffing and recruiting has significant implications for the industry, as well as for job seekers and society as a whole. While these technologies have the potential to improve the efficiency and accuracy of the hiring process, they also raise important ethical, legal, and practical challenges.

Companies must ensure that their AI and automation tools are designed and implemented in a way that is fair, unbiased, and compliant with applicable laws and regulations. They must also invest in training and upskilling their employees to effectively use and manage these tools, and be prepared to adapt their talent management strategies to account for changes in job roles and responsibilities.

Job seekers must also be prepared to develop new skills and competencies to succeed in an increasingly automated and AI-powered job market, and must be mindful of the potential impact of AI and automation on the candidate experience and diversity and inclusion issues.

As the staffing and recruiting industry continues to evolve and adapt to new technologies, it will be important for all stakeholders to work together to ensure that AI and automation are used in a responsible and effective way, to promote a fair, diverse, and sustainable workforce for the future.

TWELVE

LEADERSHIP IN STAFFING AND RECRUITING

> *"Leadership is not about being in charge. It's about taking care of those in your charge." - Simon Sinek*

Leadership in staffing and recruiting is crucial in building and leading high-performing teams. Leaders are responsible for selecting and retaining top talent that can help the organization achieve its goals. Successful staffing and recruiting strategies can help businesses gain a competitive edge, but it requires a strategic approach to identify, attract, and retain the right talent. This chapter will discuss the importance of leadership in staffing and recruiting and provide tips on how to build and lead high-performing teams.

The Importance of Leadership in Staffing and Recruiting

Leadership plays a vital role in staffing and recruiting because it sets the tone for the organization's culture and values. Leaders who prioritize recruiting and hiring the best candidates create a positive work environment that fosters productivity, collaboration, and innovation. Conversely, poor leadership in staffing and recruiting can result in high turnover rates, low employee morale, and a negative impact on the bottom line.

Effective leaders in staffing and recruiting understand the importance of identifying and attracting top talent. They prioritize diversity and inclusion in the hiring process and ensure that their recruitment strategies align with the organization's goals and values. A strong recruitment and staffing strategy should be grounded in a clear understanding of the company's objectives, culture, and industry.

How to Build and Lead High-Performing Teams

1. **Define the Role**

Before you begin the recruiting process, it's important to define the role you're hiring for. A clear job description outlining the responsibilities, qualifications, and expectations for the position will help you attract the right candidates. Be sure to involve stakeholders in the process to ensure that everyone is on the same page.

2. **Identify Top Talent**

Identifying top talent requires a strategic approach. Some of the most effective ways to find top talent include:

- Employee Referrals: Employee referrals are an excellent source of top talent because they already know and understand the organization's culture and values.

- Networking: Networking is a valuable tool for finding top talent, especially in industries with a tight labor market.
- Social Media: Social media platforms like LinkedIn and Twitter are useful for finding top talent and engaging with potential candidates.
- Job Boards: Job boards like Indeed and Monster are great resources for finding top talent.

3. **Prioritize Diversity and Inclusion**

A diverse and inclusive workforce is crucial for building a high-performing team. Leaders should prioritize diversity and inclusion in the hiring process by:

- Creating diverse hiring teams
- Removing bias from the hiring process
- Writing inclusive job descriptions
- Offering unconscious bias training to employees

4. **Use Behavioral Interviewing**

Behavioral interviewing is an effective way to assess a candidate's past behavior and predict their future performance. Behavioral interview questions ask candidates to describe specific situations they've faced in the past and how they handled them. By asking candidates to describe their behavior in specific situations, you can gain insight into their problem-solving skills, communication style, and decision-making abilities.

5. **Offer Competitive Compensation and Benefits**

Offering competitive compensation and benefits is crucial for attracting and retaining top talent. Leaders should research industry standards and ensure that their compensation packages are competitive. Benefits like health insurance, retirement plans, and flexible work arrangements are also essential for attracting and retaining top talent.

6. **Provide Opportunities for Growth and Development**

Top talent wants to work for organizations that prioritize growth and development. Leaders should offer opportunities for professional development, mentorship programs, and career advancement. Providing employees with opportunities to grow and develop their skills will help them feel valued and invested in the organization's success.

7. **Communicate Clearly and Effectively**

Clear and effective communication is essential for building a high-performing team. Leaders should communicate clearly and frequently with their team members, providing feedback and recognition when appropriate. Regular check-ins with team members can help leaders identify potential issues and address them before they become problems.

8. **Foster a Positive Work Environment**

A positive work environment is crucial for building a high-performing team. Leaders should prioritize creating a workplace culture that values open communication, collaboration, and respect. This can be achieved by:

- Encouraging team members to share their ideas and opinions
- Providing opportunities for team members to collaborate on projects
- Offering team-building activities and social events
- Recognizing and rewarding team members for their hard work and achievements

9. **Lead by Example**

Leadership in staffing and recruiting requires leading by example. Leaders should model the behavior they want to see in their team members, demonstrating the organization's values and priorities. Leaders should also be transparent and accountable, taking responsibility for their actions and decisions.

10. **Continuously Improve and Adapt**

Building and leading a high-performing team is an ongoing process that requires continuous improvement and adaptation. Leaders should regularly assess their staffing and recruiting strategies, identifying areas for improvement and making changes as needed. This can include:

- Gathering feedback from team members
- Analysing recruitment and retention data
- Staying up to date with industry trends and best practices

Conclusion

Leadership in staffing and recruiting is essential for building and leading high-performing teams. Effective leaders prioritize identifying and attracting top talent, fostering a positive work environment, and continuously improving and adapting their strategies. By following these tips, leaders can create a workplace culture that values diversity, collaboration, and innovation, ultimately driving the organization's success.

THIRTEEN

THE ROLE OF DATA ANALYTICS IN STAFFING AND RECRUITING

> *"Data is the new oil. It's valuable, but if unrefined it cannot really be used." - Clive Humby*

The role of data analytics in staffing and recruiting has become increasingly important in recent years. With the rise of big data and the proliferation of digital technologies, companies can now collect and analyze vast amounts of data about job candidates, employee performance, and workforce trends. By leveraging this data, companies can make better-informed staffing and recruiting decisions, resulting in better outcomes for both the company and its employees.

This paper will explore the role of data analytics in staffing and recruiting, including its benefits, challenges, and best practices. We will also discuss some of the key trends in data analytics and how they are shaping the future of staffing and recruiting.

Benefits of Data Analytics in Staffing and Recruiting:

There are several benefits of using data analytics in staffing and recruiting, including:

- **Improved Hiring Decisions:** Data analytics can help companies make more informed hiring decisions by providing insights into a candidate's skills, qualifications, and fit for the role. By analyzing data from resumes, job applications, and assessments, companies can identify candidates who are likely to succeed in the role and avoid those who may not be a good fit.

- **Better Retention:** Data analytics can also help companies identify factors that contribute to employee turnover, such as job satisfaction, work-life balance, and compensation. By analyzing this data, companies can make changes to improve employee retention and reduce turnover.

- **Increased Efficiency:** Data analytics can help companies streamline their recruiting processes by automating tasks such as resume screening and scheduling interviews. This can save time and resources, allowing recruiters to focus on more strategic tasks such as building relationships with candidates.

- **Improved Diversity:** Data analytics can also help companies improve their diversity and inclusion efforts by identifying biases in the recruiting process and providing insights into how to overcome them. For example, by analyzing data on the demographics of job applicants and hires, companies can identify areas where they need to improve their recruiting efforts to attract a more diverse pool of candidates.

Challenges of Data Analytics in Staffing and Recruiting:

While there are many benefits to using data analytics in staffing and recruiting, there are also several challenges that companies must overcome to fully leverage the power of data. These challenges include:

- **Data Quality:** One of the biggest challenges in using data analytics for staffing and recruiting is ensuring that the data is accurate, complete, and relevant. This requires companies to have systems in place to collect and store data effectively, as well as processes for cleaning and validating the data.

- **Privacy and Security:** Another challenge is ensuring the privacy and security of candidate data. Companies must comply with data protection regulations such as GDPR and CCPA, as well as ensuring that candidate data is stored securely and accessed only by authorized personnel.

- **Skill and Resource Gaps:** Many companies lack the necessary skills and resources to effectively use data analytics for staffing and recruiting. This may require investing in training and development for existing staff or hiring data analytics specialists to fill skill gaps.

- **Bias:** Data analytics can also perpetuate biases in the recruiting process if the data being analyzed is biased. For example, if historical data shows that certain demographics are more successful in certain roles, this may lead to bias in the recruiting process. It is essential to ensure that data is not biased and that any biases are identified and addressed.

Best Practices for Using Data Analytics in Staffing and Recruiting:

To fully leverage the benefits of data analytics in staffing and recruiting, companies should follow some best practices, including:

- **Defining Clear Objectives:** It is important to define clear objectives for data analytics projects, such as improving candidate quality or reducing time-to-hire. This ensures that the data being analyzed is relevant and useful.

- **Collecting Quality Data:** To ensure the accuracy and relevance of the data being analyzed, companies must have effective systems in place to collect and store data. This includes ensuring that the data is complete, accurate, and consistent, and that it is stored securely.

- **Cleaning and Validating Data:** Before analyzing data, it is important to clean and validate it to ensure that it is accurate and reliable. This includes removing duplicates, correcting errors, and ensuring that data is consistent across different sources.

- **Using the Right Tools and Techniques:** Companies should use the right tools and techniques to analyze data, such as machine learning algorithms, natural language processing, and data visualization tools. This can help to uncover patterns and insights that may not be visible using traditional analysis techniques.

- **Involving Stakeholders:** To ensure that data analytics projects are aligned with business objectives and are effective, it is important to involve stakeholders, including recruiters, hiring managers, and HR professionals. This can help to ensure that data analytics projects are focused on the right objectives and that the results are actionable.

- **Monitoring and Iterating:** Data analytics projects should be monitored and iterated over time to ensure that they remain relevant and effective. This may involve adjusting the data being analyzed, refining analysis techniques, or changing the objectives of the project.

Trends in Data Analytics in Staffing and Recruiting:

There are several key trends in data analytics in staffing and recruiting that are shaping the future of the industry. These trends include:

- **Predictive Analytics:** Predictive analytics involves using data to predict future outcomes, such as which candidates are most likely to succeed in a role or which employees are at risk of leaving the company. Predictive analytics can help companies make more informed decisions about hiring and retention.

- **Artificial Intelligence and Machine Learning:** Artificial intelligence and machine learning are increasingly being used in staffing and recruiting to automate tasks such as resume screening, scheduling interviews, and even conducting interviews. This can save time and resources and improve the quality of hiring decisions.

- **Data-Driven Diversity and Inclusion:** Data analytics can help companies improve their diversity and inclusion efforts by identifying areas where they need to improve their recruiting efforts and by providing insights into how to overcome biases in the recruiting process.

- **Real-Time Analytics:** Real-time analytics involves analyzing data as it is generated, such as social media posts or online job applications. Real-time analytics can help companies identify trends and insights as they are happening, allowing them to make more informed decisions about hiring and retention.

Conclusion:

The role of data analytics in staffing and recruiting is becoming increasingly important in today's data-driven business environment. By leveraging data, companies can make better-informed hiring and retention decisions, resulting in better outcomes for both the company and its employees. However, there are also several challenges that must be overcome, such as ensuring the accuracy and relevance of data, addressing biases, and complying with data protection regulations. To fully leverage the benefits of data analytics, companies must follow best practices such as defining clear objectives, collecting quality data, and using the right tools and techniques. As data analytics continues to evolve, companies that can effectively leverage data will have a competitive advantage in the staffing and recruiting industry.

FOURTEEN

THE FUTURE OF STAFFING AND RECRUITING

> *"The staffing industry must adapt to the changing workforce dynamics, including the rise of remote work, the gig economy, and the demand for more flexible work arrangements."*

Staffing and recruiting is a vital aspect of any organization, as it is responsible for finding and retaining top talent that can drive the organization's success. With the rise of technology and data analytics, the staffing and recruiting industry is rapidly evolving. This chapter explores the future of staffing and recruiting, including trends and predictions for the industry.

1. **Virtual Recruiting:**

One of the biggest trends in the staffing and recruiting industry is virtual recruiting. Virtual recruiting refers to the use of technology to conduct recruiting activities remotely. This can include conducting virtual job fairs, video interviews, and online assessments.

The COVID-19 pandemic has accelerated the adoption of virtual recruiting, as companies had to adapt to remote work and social distancing guidelines. Virtual recruiting has several benefits, including the ability to reach a wider pool of candidates and reducing recruiting costs. It also allows companies to hire from anywhere in the world, making it easier to find top talent.

Virtual recruiting is likely to continue to grow in the future, even after the pandemic subsides. Companies will continue to use virtual recruiting to attract and retain top talent, and it will become an integral part of the recruiting process.

1. **Artificial Intelligence:**

Artificial intelligence (AI) is already being used in staffing and recruiting to automate tasks such as resume screening and scheduling interviews. AI can help to reduce time and resources spent on recruiting, and it can also improve the quality of hiring decisions.

In the future, AI is likely to become even more prevalent in staffing and recruiting. For example, AI could be used to analyze social media profiles to identify potential candidates, or it could be used to predict which candidates are most likely to succeed in a role.

However, there are also concerns about the use of AI in recruiting, particularly around bias and discrimination. Companies will need to be careful to ensure that AI is used ethically and that it does not perpetuate existing biases in the recruiting process.

3. **Data Analytics:**

Data analytics is another trend that is already transforming the staffing and recruiting industry. By leveraging data, companies can make more informed decisions about hiring and retention, resulting in better outcomes for both the company and its employees.

In the future, data analytics is likely to become even more important in staffing and recruiting. Predictive analytics, for example, could be used to identify which candidates are most likely to succeed in a role, or which employees are at risk of leaving the company. Real-time analytics could be used to identify trends and insights as they are happening, allowing companies to make more informed decisions about hiring and retention.

However, as with AI, there are also concerns about data analytics in recruiting, particularly around privacy and data protection. Companies will need to ensure that they are collecting and using data ethically, and that they are complying with relevant data protection regulations.

4. **Soft Skills:**

Soft skills, such as communication and problem-solving, have always been important in the workplace. However, as technology and automation continue to reshape the workplace, soft skills are becoming even more important.

In the future, soft skills are likely to become a key focus of recruiting and talent development. Companies will need to find ways to identify and develop soft skills in their employees, as they will be critical for success in a rapidly changing workplace.

5. **Diversity and Inclusion:**

Diversity and inclusion have become increasingly important in the workplace, and this trend is likely to continue in the future. Companies will need to find ways to attract and retain diverse talent, and to create an inclusive workplace culture.

Data analytics can be used to help companies improve their diversity and inclusion efforts. For example, data analytics can be used to identify areas where companies need to improve their recruiting efforts, or to provide insights into how to overcome biases in the recruiting process.

6. **Employer Branding:**

Employer branding refers to the reputation that a company has as an employer. It includes factors such as company culture, values, and benefits, and it is becoming increasingly important in the recruiting process.

In the future, employer branding is likely to become even more important as companies compete for top talent. Companies will need to find ways to differentiate themselves from their competitors and to communicate their employer brand effectively to potential candidates.

Social media and online platforms will continue to play a critical role in employer branding, as candidates increasingly use these platforms to research potential employers. Companies will need to have a strong online presence and a clear employer brand message to attract top talent.

7. **Gig Economy:**

The gig economy refers to the trend of workers taking on short-term or freelance work, rather than traditional full-time employment. This trend has been growing in recent years, and it is likely to continue in the future.

For companies, the gig economy can provide access to a wider pool of talent and greater flexibility in hiring. However, it also presents challenges in terms of managing and retaining gig workers.

In the future, companies will need to find ways to effectively manage gig workers and to create a positive experience for them. This could include offering flexible work arrangements, providing training and development opportunities, and ensuring that gig workers are integrated into the company culture.

8. **Remote Work:**

The COVID-19 pandemic has accelerated the trend of remote work, and it is likely to continue in the future. Remote work provides greater flexibility for both employers and employees, and it can also reduce costs associated with office space and commuting.

For staffing and recruiting, remote work presents both challenges and opportunities. Companies will need to find ways to effectively recruit and manage remote workers, and to ensure that they are able to collaborate effectively with team members.

However, remote work also presents opportunities for companies to recruit top talent from anywhere in the world, and to create a more diverse and inclusive workforce.

9. **Employee Experience:**

Employee experience refers to the overall experience that an employee has with a company, from the recruiting process through to their ongoing employment. It includes factors such as company culture, benefits, and work-life balance.

In the future, employee experience is likely to become even more important in the recruiting process. Candidates will be looking for companies that offer a positive employee experience, and companies will need to find ways to differentiate themselves in this area.

Data analytics can be used to help companies improve their employee experience, by identifying areas where improvements can be made and providing insights into how to create a positive workplace culture.

10. **Continuous Learning:**

Continuous learning refers to the ongoing process of learning and development that takes place throughout an employee's career. In the rapidly changing workplace, continuous learning is becoming increasingly important, as employees need to keep up with new technologies and skills.

In the future, companies will need to find ways to provide ongoing learning and development opportunities for their employees, and to create a culture of continuous learning. This could include offering online training programs, providing mentorship and coaching, and encouraging employees to attend conferences and events.

Conclusion:

The staffing and recruiting industry is rapidly evolving, driven by technology, data analytics, and changing workplace trends. In the future, virtual recruiting, artificial intelligence, data analytics, soft skills, diversity and inclusion, employer branding, the gig economy, remote work, employee experience, and continuous learning will all be key trends in the industry.

Companies that are able to effectively leverage these trends will be better positioned to attract and retain top talent, and to drive success in the rapidly changing workplace.

Printed by Libri Plureos GmbH in Hamburg,
Germany